YOUR CHALK CAN TALK

YOUR CHALK CAN TALK

by

JERRY ZWALL

MOODY PRESS

CHICAGO

ACKNOWLEDGMENT

I wish to express my sincere thanks for the encouragement I received from many who are interested in presenting the gospel of the Lord Jesus Christ through the use of chalk drawings.

My appreciation to these in particular: Elmer L. Wilder, Phil Saint, Art Layne and Karl Steele.

ISBN: 0-8024-9850-7

10th Printing, 1979

INTRODUCTION

Those who are aware of the value of visual aids in presenting gospel truths will be lastingly appreciative of Mr. Zwall for this splendid book, *Your Chalk Can Talk*. Many who have had the desire to thus illustrate Bible truths and have felt an inability to do so will be forever grateful. With the aid of this book they can become practical if not professional in causing chalk to talk.

With a long and effective background of art, visual evangelism and theological training, Mr. Zwall is eminently qualified to author a book such as this one. The simplicity of the illustrations and the explicitness of instructions will cause many to stop wishing and start working in the great task of illustrating the eternal truths of the Word of God.

It need not be said of those who read and heed the pages of this book, "The young children ask bread and no man breaketh it unto them" (Lamentations 4:4).

ELMER L. WILDER, Th. D.

CONTENTS

A WORD TO BEGIN

Have you ever watched a chalk artist as he presented the gospel in beautiful colors, and wished you too could have the same ability?

"But I just can't draw!" This seems to be the attitude of many. If you make up your mind that you "just can't draw," you perhaps never will. Let's take the "t" out of "can't" and make it "I can draw."

I believe you can give a successful chalk-talk, and the purpose of this book is to make that a reality. Use it as a guide. The pen drawings enclosed will be a help to get started. Do not become addicted to copying, but rather try to develop originality. Use the ideas, but, as my homiletics professor often warned, "put your own meat on the bones."

I realize that the entire scope of chalk-talk information is far too broad to be covered in a book such as this. But because of many inquiries, I feel that the ideas I have gathered over the years should be passed on.

As you take up the challenge to do chalk-talks, remember this: All the Lord asks is your heart, your mind and eyes wide awake to observe, and your yielded hands to be guilded by Him.

My prayer is that you may "draw" from His storehouse the thrill of doing chalk-talks.

SIMPLE GOSPEL ILLUSTRATIONS

On the opposite page are your easel, newsprint paper, and a piece of black chalk. The drawing requires no special ability. It is a springboard for the greatest subject on earth. Please take up the challenge and share in the joy of "drawing" precious souls to Christ.

Keep the drawing plain and simple. Omit the drawing of the Bible, if you wish, but be sure to give the Scripture reference. Now draw that hill. Put in the three crosses. Talk as you draw. The jets, or stick figures, are easy. A little practice in preparation (see p. 46-47), and you will do them well.

Don't overdo a good thing. For your Sunday school class or Bible club, one chalk-talk a month or one every two weeks is advisable. The attention will be 100 percent, and your class will eagerly anticipate your next chalk-talk.

On the following pages are drawings that you can do, with an explanation for each. Pick out one to fit your lesson and *do* it. One must make a start sometime. Keep in mind the lasting impression your lesson will have with your chalk-talk. A bit crude? Perhaps. But most who are using chalk-talks successfully, started this way. After struggling through my first, I was asked, "What is it?" Had I quit then, you would not be reading this.

It is not our purpose to discredit the tremendous value of the flannelgraph or the blackboard. Your chalk-talks, however, will bring a fresh approach to the gospel. Because something is being created before your class, you will be assured of good attention. Chalk-talks are indelibly impressed upon the minds of those who watch. One day I was sitting in the waiting room of a doctor's office. A man entered with a boy about six years of age. Suddenly, to my embarrassment, the boy pointed to me among those waiting and burst out, "Dad, there's the man who drew the mule!" Although I did not recognize the lad, I did remember giving a chalk-talk on stubbornness at a nearby Sunday school.

1

2

3

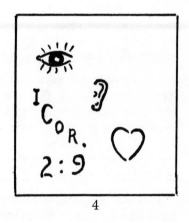

4

5

6

1

1. Draw the cylinder (use red, if possible, then outline with black).
2. Put fuse in.
3. Write in the reference, Romans 1:16, and quote the verse.
4. Tell about use of dynamite.
5. Draw explosion as you tell how hard hearts can be broken by the gospel.

2

1. Draw upper part of head.
2. Tell of boy in trouble, unsaved.
3. Draw two long lines down for nose.
4. Boy is invited to Sunday school and receives Christ.
5. Now draw top of Bible first and finish with reference and change in boy's life.

3

1. Draw cross and tell of the tree of Calvary and gift of salvation.
2. Draw gift package and tell of receiving gift.
3. Write reference.

4

1. Draw the eye and tell what we are able to see — beauty, etc.
2. Draw ear and tell about beautiful sounds — music, etc.
3. Draw heart and tell of mind, knowledge and emotions.
4. Write in verse and tell of heaven.

5

1. Draw sad face and speak of sin and its results.
2. Put in lines above eyes and write in II Corinthians 5:17.
3. Tell about the old things and the new things.
4. Tear off and show smiling face drawn previously on sheet behind.

6

1. Say, "Let's play a game. What is the number?"
2. Draw in numbers 1-11, as shown, and make a comment about each.
3. Conclude by asking if their lives count for Christ.

7

8

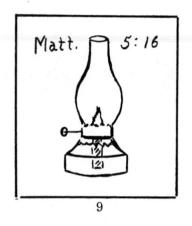

9

10

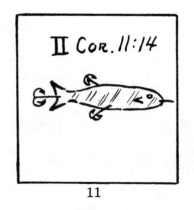

11

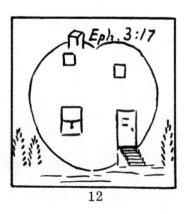

12

14

1. Draw distant hill, the city, and "ETERNAL LIFE."
2. Tell of heaven, our future home.
3. Draw the wall of sin (three lines — use perspective).
4. Tell of sin that separates, and put in the ladders: W — works; $ — wealth; R — religion; E — education; P — popularity.
5. Draw cross in red, the path and the burdened one.
6. Mention that efforts are acceptable on the other side.

1. Draw just the pole, faith.
2. Next the line, love.
3. The weight, prayer.
4. The hook, the Holy Spirit.
5. The bait, God's Word.
6. The verse, Matthew 4:19.

1. Draw the globe — It must be clean.
2. The base — It must be kept filled (with the Spirit).
3. Regulator — Let Christ run our lives.
4. Write the verse, Matthew 5:16.

1. "I am the bread of life" (John 6:35).
2. Discuss food and mention Jeremiah 15:16.
3. Draw the loaves and read John 6:9.

1. Draw fish, using many bright colors. "Did you ever see a fish like this?"
2. Draw in the hooks and line.
3. Put in verse and tell of Satan's tricks. Hooks represent many things.

1. Draw the heart-house telling of the man who invited a traveler in.
2. The traveler's name was Sin.
3. Trouble followed.
4. Jesus was invited in and cleaned the house.

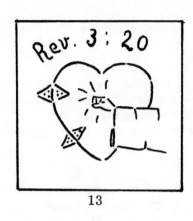

13

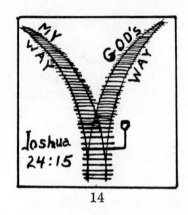

14

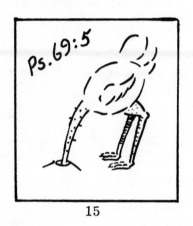

15

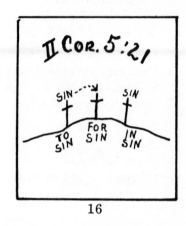

16

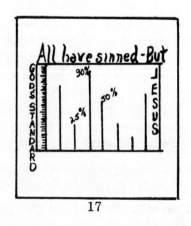

17

18

16

1. Draw the heart. Remember to skip space for the arm. This is an unusual heart.
2. Put in hinges. It is a door.
3. Draw hand knocking, and write in verse.
4. Discuss opening door and many rooms.

1. In perspective draw the four main lines.
2. As you put in ties, tell of the two ways.
3. Approaching the switch, we decide. Choose the right way.
4. Put in "MY WAY" and "GOD'S WAY."
5. Write in Joshua 24:15 as you quote it.

1. Draw ostrich.
2. Write Psalm 69:5. Many try to hide from their sins.
3. "Be sure your sin will find you out" (Numbers 32:23) and related verses.

1. Draw the line for the hill.
2. The cross to the right — tell of his sin and his death (*in* sin).
3. The left cross — tell of his dying request (dead *to* sin).
4. The center cross — Christ died *for* sin.

1. Draw bottom line, top line and the measure. Write and discuss "GOD'S STANDARD."
2. Tell of many human efforts and failure.
3. "ALL HAVE SINNED — BUT."
4. Draw in line that reaches (JESUS).

1. Put in two cliffs. Leave space open for cross.
2. Draw buildings; dots for windows; flames.
3. Tell of gulf caused by sin.
4. Put in cross and distant scene. "How shall we escape, if we neglect . . . ?" (Hebrews 2:3). "I am the way, the truth, and the life" (John 14:6).

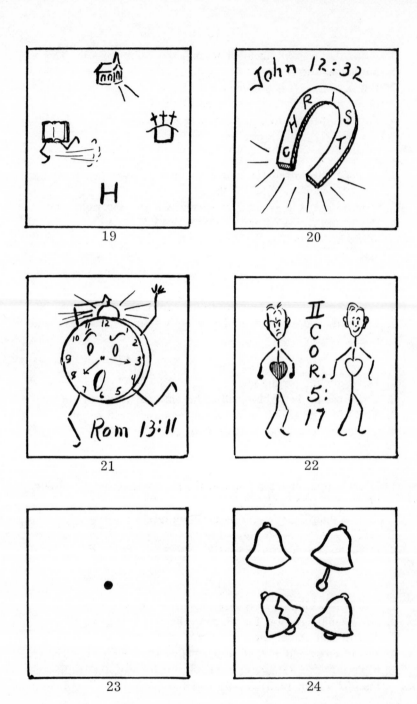

19

20

21

22

23

24

1. Draw "H," just the square under crosses, a square side of church and the square center of the Bible. Discuss baseball.
2. First base — salvation. We must touch first in God's game. Put in crosses.
3. Draw church out of square. Second base — worship, Bible study, prayer.
4. Third base — service. Make Bible out of square.
4. H stands for home base or heaven.

20

1. Draw magnet. Discuss its uses.
2. Print in "C-H-R-I-S-T" and give the verse.

21

1. Draw circle first, alarm on top, then 12, 6, 9, 3, and fill in the rest.
2. Put on arms and legs indicating urgency. Discuss various kinds of clocks. How many minutes are in a year? Answer: 525,600. How many are used for the Lord?
3. Give verse.

22

1. Draw dark heart and figure. Tell of nature of sin and results.
2. Draw white heart and figure. Tell of old things that pass away.
3. Give the verse, II Corinthians 5:17.

23

1. Here is the easiest of all chalk-talks. Just a dot.
2. Ask, "What do you see? Oh, you see a dot? Is that all?"
3. Object: Don't always look for the dark things. Most of the paper is white.
4. Explain II Corinthians 4:18.

24

1. Draw four bells. Tell of Liberty Bell; bells of salvation — Exodus 28:33-34; bells of victory — Zechariah 14:20.
2. No clapper — dumbbell. Long clapper — long tongue. Cracked bell — uncertain testimony. Good bell.

25

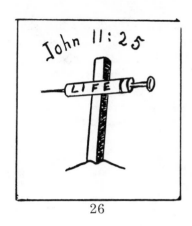

26

27

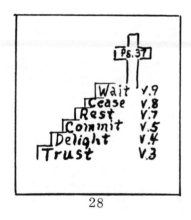

28

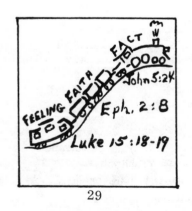

29

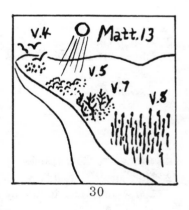

30

25

1. Draw the signs. Discuss man's way.
2. Put in the confused traveler.
3. Write in verse and explain. Also mention John 14:6.

26

1. Draw hypodermic needle (color in red — print in "LIFE"). Ask class about shots. Tell of life-giving serum.
2. Put in post to form cross and tell of the serum of Calvary and eternal life.
3. Speak of verse, John 11:25.

27

1. Draw green tree. (A simple chalk-talk for Christmastime. Use color if possible.)
2. Put in cross (I Peter 2:24 goes well here).
3. At the tree of Calvary is a gift for all. Draw box and arm (Christ the Giver).
4. Draw in verse.

28

1. Here is a good study of Psalm 37:1-9. Beforehand, draw the steps only.
2. Begin with "Trust" — first step. Ask if each has trusted.
3. "Delight," "Commit," "Rest," "Cease," and "Wait."
4. Draw the cross.

29

1. Draw track first.
2. Draw engine, cars and caboose. Talk about toy trains, etc.
3. Write "Fact," "Faith" and "Feeling." Caboose has no power. Cars so often empty. These must depend on engine (Facts).
3. Write in the verses for each.

30

1. Draw three lines, path and horizon.
2. Write in Matthew 13. Draw seed and birds — explain verse 4.
3. Seed, rocks and sun — explain verse 5.
4. Seed and thorns — explain verse 7.
5. Good harvest, good soil — explain verse 8.

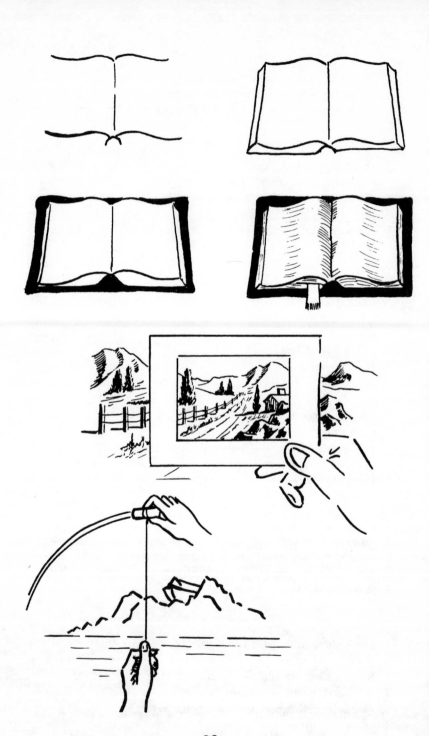

COLORED CHALK-TALKS TO TRY

I have sketched twelve of my most used colored chalk-talks. I hope you will try them. Opposite each of these I have given some suggestions as to color, light and shade. Develop the use of the broad side of your chalk. This will speed up your work. Remember, no details. Stand approximately two-thirds of your arm length from your board. Don't crowd too close. As much as possible, draw from the side. Try placing your chalk tray to the side of your easel. This will give your group a full view each time you select a piece of chalk.

Line your chalks up before you start. Always check your lights. Have your blending eraser ready. Now, start with that sky. Use bold, sweeping strokes. Now that billowy cloud. Get going and learn that your chalk can talk.

THE THREE CROSSES

The sky could be a dark blue. Billowy clouds showing a disturbing movement would help. Just behind the crosses have a brilliant sky, ultraviolet, if used. Distant hills, light purple. City, solid white first. Note source of light, and shade buildings, using deep blue or deep purple. Green field. Small trees in black. Rocky hill, solid gray or brick-brown. Highlight with ultraviolet and shade with dark blue. Little green on path. Black spruce in foreground. Three crosses black against brilliant sky.

THREE WISE MEN

Deep blue sky with a little streak of light blue on the horizon (ultraviolet). Purple distant hills. White buildings. Dark green fields. Dark brown path. Foreground all in solid black (silhouette), including wise men. Highlight, yellow plain or ultraviolet. Star (ultraviolet) yellow or white.

WAY OF THE CROSS

First, city in white (ultraviolet). Shade buildings blue. Black trees. Dark blue billowy clouds first, then lighter blue as you come down. Highlight, yellow or white (ultraviolet). Broad sweeps of flare-red (ultraviolet) at the bottom. World, solid light blue (ultraviolet), black land mass. Cross, white (ultraviolet) with deep purple shading. Watch perspective. White dots for stars (ultraviolet).

BURDEN AT THE CROSS

Plain blue sky. Large billowy ultraviolet yellow or white cloud, shaded with light blue. Figure and hill, all black. Cross, ultraviolet white and shaded with dark blue.

EMPTY TOMB

Sky, your choice, but keep sky bright behind three crosses. Dark green hill. Brown path. Dark gray rocks shaded with blue or purple. Highlight, bright yellow. Tree black or deep green. Shade tree trunk darkest.

THE WAY OF ESCAPE

Graduate distant sky from dark blue to brilliant yellow. Skip the bridge, however. Brown cliffs on each side. Purple from middle of cliffs to bottom of paper. Blend into brown. City of death black with ultraviolet dots. Yellow and red flames. Black smoke. City of life white. Shade blue. Black trees. Bridge gray. People black. Highlight cliffs, yellow. Print "DEATH," "LIFE," "SIN" and "JESUS."

LIGHTHOUSE ON BIBLE

Plain mottled sky. Streak blue and white and blend with blending eraser. Draw Bible (ultraviolet white pages, yellow edges), gray rocks, blue (ultraviolet), shaded side of waves, white (ultraviolet), light side of waves. Lighthouse (ultraviolet), white shaded blue. Brilliant light (ultraviolet). Black top and windows. Shade rocks.

I AM THE WAY

Light blue sky. Billowy clouds (plain chalk). Ultraviolet city. Light purple cliffs (bold downstrokes). Black trees. Ultraviolet cross with dark blue shading (remember perspective). Black jet figures. Black Bible edge (start at top). Yellow ultraviolet page edges.

IT IS FINISHED

Plain blue sky. Billowy ultraviolet white or yellow cloud and light blue shading. Foreground, black silhouette.

30

PASSOVER

Plain deep blue sky. Distant hills brown. Pyramid, light touch of ultraviolet shaded with light blue. Plain white buildings and wall (use broadside of chalk). Dark green foreground. Black trees, highlighted. Red ultraviolet spots on doors. (Draw in red, ultraviolet cross in the door while black light is on.)

WHITER THAN SNOW

Plain light blue sky. Use white first on mountains. Light purple shading on distant mountains, darker purple on others. White snowfields (broad strokes). With edge of purple make short up- or downstrokes for shaded snowbank. Blue for water, streaked with white. A touch of green at edge of stream. Black trees. Highlight.

LIGHTHOUSE

With plain chalk, graduate sky from dark blue down to a flesh and a soft stroke of yellow ultraviolet. Solid ultraviolet blue sea. With broadside of ultraviolet white, put in long breakers with perspective. Rocky cliff and rock, gray with purple shading and bright highlight (ultraviolet). For lighthouse and building, ultraviolet white shaded with light blue. For dashing waves use circular motion with ultraviolet white.

IT TOOK A TREE

When God first sought to tell to men the story
Of His creative might, He fashioned trees—
Tall spires of green that published forth
His glory,
Great pines on rock ledges by the seas.
He gave His beauty in abundant measure
To palms and willows eloquent with shade,
To blossoms speaking of the harvest
treasure . . .
And called it good, the things that He had
made.

But when in grace His Father-heart was
burning
To tell to men His love, the trees were still;
They had no word to speak the holy yearning . . .
It took a tree uplifted on a hill.
It took a Cross with biting nails and crown
To tell God's love and bring redemption
down.

RUTH GIBBS ZWALL
in *War Cry*

32

SUBJECTS TO PRACTICE

TREES

From the tree of life in the garden, to the tree of life in glory, trees have been of great importance to man's existence. I trust you will be led of God to "draw" precious souls to the tree of Calvary.

Let us consider trees in our chalk drawings. Keep in mind that each tree has its own special shape, and it is important to know each line involved. To those drawn in this book, add your own sketches of other trees. When bare of leaves, their form can be studied more easily. Train yourself to have a mental picture of trees. The type of tree is often quickly detected by how and where the limbs leave the trunk.

Because of limited time for chalk-talks, one must draw masses of color. This may be brilliant yellow or rust for autumn, light blue or light purple for distant evergreen or deciduous trees. Dark green masses for nearby cone-shaped hemlock or spruce. For the very close foreground, deep dark green or even black can be used. These graded colors will provide the perspective needed. The above-mentioned should be highlighted and shaded. The shaded areas are usually done in masses of deep colors.

Always observe the source of light. Ground shadows are important. Try the upward stroke for limbs and twigs. Practice twisting your chalk from broad to very thin. This works especially well on palm trees. Try the stipple method for autumn leaves, using yellow, red and rust. Keep in mind that certain areas require different types of trees. For a fringe of evergreen trees, draw with short up- and downstrokes. If these are along a lake, pull down the chalk into the water with your finger. This will give you the reflection (see illustration).

33

37

BOATS AND SHIPS

"There go the ships," said the psalmist in Psalm 104:26. What a variety of ships and boats the Bible tells of. Look them up; hoist the sail. Let's go fishing and "draw" in the net for the Lord.

I have drawn a few boats for you to practice. File your own sketches. Avoid details. What rich subjects to draw:

Rescue the Perishing
Shipwreck
Fishing for Jesus
Noah's Ark
Jonah
Disciples in the Storm
Peace Be Still

Bon voyage!

FIGURE DRAWING

In Mark 8:24 we read of a man who had distorted vision. He saw "men as trees, walking." By the touch of our wonderful Lord he was made to see "clearly" (v. 25). In the subject before us it is important to be clear in our drawing of figures and avoid distortion.

It is my advice for beginners not to attempt drawing figures in public. If any are done, it should be merely suggestion. By this, I mean drawing only side views of heads or using a dark silhouette. One *must* be very sure of body proportions. Keep this in mind constantly.

In your practice of figures, encourage others to criticize your work. Practice figures in silhouette. Remember the rules of proportion: for a man, approximately eight heads; for a woman, approximately seven heads; the face, approximately the length of the hand; eyes, in center of head. Ears are approximately from the eyebrow to the bottom of the nose. Be sure to check length of hand to length of face.

Practice this technique:
1. Draw a figure using sketchy style with only essential details.
2. Fill in solid with one dark tone. Now you have your dark tones.
3. Sketch in all the highlights next. Remember source of light.
4. Draw in the medium tones next.
5. Over this use any other color necessary to darken the shades or brighten the highlights.

Lecture crayon is the answer to the "color wheel confusion." Just choose the color you feel is best. Add white for lighter color, and black, purple or dark brown for darker tones. To give a smoothness, use finger or blending felt.

HIGHLIGHT AND SHADOW

The Christian experience is filled with shadows and lights. Jesus Christ is our great source of light. Often, as in Psalm 23, we walk in the shadows. However, with every shadow there must be a light. Bear in mind that this applies to artwork also.

Your chalk picture will appear real when highlights and shadows are properly used. This will keep your picture from being monotonous and flat.

The gradual shading on the lighthouse, tree or fence post will give it the round look. It also gives strength and dimension to rocks. Keep in mind that for distant objects delicate shadows are used. That distant mountain, cloud or wave needs a light shading. Objects in the foreground require stronger shade colors. The surrounding area and close objects have an effect on all of this. Reflected light from a nearby rock or building should show up in the shadow.

A good practice subject for shade variation would be to shine a strong floodlight on a ball. Notice the highlight, the gradual shading, the cast shadow and, if there is an object nearby, the reflected light.

Always remember the source of light.

CLOUDS

Here again is a thrilling subject for you to experience. Clouds can be drawn in great variety. Job said, "Who can number the clouds?" (Job 38:37). I challenge you to do a scene with a billowy white cloud and gather from your Bible "showers" of blessed truths. Consider the bow in the cloud — God's promise. Or the cloud of God's presence, power and protection for His people as they traveled. Think of His ascension and of His coming.

Draw a cloud. It gives action to your drawing. Study the various formations and color value. Your cloud should fit your land or seascape. Clouds should lend the feeling of peace, judgment, storm, wind, beauty, distance, etc.

Always remember source of light and, of course, the shading. Don't overdo on highlight and shading. Try blending (hard) with your hand, in circular motion. For a "sweeping sky," use the broadside of your chalk in long, bold strokes.

Never let your clouds distract from your central theme. On a dark gray cloud, try rubbing some of the light highlight back into the dark area. This will give you a shaft of light. Or, in reverse, pull down some of the dark into the light area. This will suggest rain in sections. Note the few sketches I have drawn. One more subject idea: Keep Looking Up (I Thessalonians 4:17).

STICK FIGURES

With very little practice one can do these simple stick figures. It will be a real challenge to draw a Bible story this way. Action can be achieved that will not only hold the interest of the class but put life in the lesson.

Use white newsprint, of course, and black or a dark colored chalk. Try the stick figures at the top of the page for practice. An oval or round dot, a line down, shoulder line under the head and arms and legs depending on the position or action of the figure.

In the second illustration, notice the Lord is not drawn. The class will soon understand this suggestion.

In the story of Jonah, one could use the last stick figure at the top of the page showing the position of running away from the Lord. The ship, the whale, the praying figure should be drawn as you tell the story.

The two men praying in the temple and the boy with the lunch will long be remembered.

The one at the bottom of the page is my favorite. David and Goliath begins with drawing the hill and valley. Draw so all the class can see. They will ask for a repeat on this one.

THE EASEL

The woman of Samaria said to Jesus, "Sir, thou hast nothing to 'draw' with, and the well is deep." She realized the need of proper equipment to draw water from the well. The privilege of drawing pictures from the deep well of God's Word requires good equipment. Those for whom you are drawing should be impressed by your equipment. Your easel should be neat and suitable to your group. It should not be overly attractive so as to distract from your picture but rather made to center their attention on the drawing. Your message is most important.

You either have or will have an easel of the "do it yourself" type. I have never seen two easels alike. Build one to meet your need. In these pages you may find a few suggestions for the construction of your easel. My first easel was a monstrosity. Several friends were always invited to go with me to carry the many parts. Through the years I have found ideas to make it more compact. Every easel should be light, compact and thus very portable.

Don't use a big bulky easel in a small room. If possible have two easels, a large one and a smaller one. The drawing area of my small easel is 30 x 30 inches and sits on a folding tripod. Be sure the tripod is sturdy and one that can fold into your box-type easel. My large easel has a drawing area of approximately 32 x 39 inches and is also adaptable for the full-size sheet of gray bogus — 40 x 54 inches.

If you use aluminum, plywood or canvas, be sure that the easel will be firm and not wobbly. Plan your easel so that it can be set up in about fifteen to twenty-five minutes. I have eight wing nuts to tighten in setting up. Study the sketches. The aluminum legs are TV aerial tubing sections and join in the center (eight pieces). The piano hinge fits the length of the easel box. Remember the folding box-type easel must have a proper slant (notice 2½ inches against 4½ inches).

Plan to have a frame — one that folds. Do not use one that is overly attractive but rather one that will enhance your drawing.

Drapes on either side of your easel will help guide attention to the picture. A light drape rod can be attached easily to the top of the box-type easel. Drape material should be plain and dark.

Some easels have a chalk tray attached to the easel just below the picture. This is very convenient for the artist. My chalk tray is placed usually to the side of the easel. This gives the viewers opportunity to see the entire picture each time I select a piece of chalk.

I have found the folding box-type easel to be very satisfactory. (My thanks to Phil Saint for suggesting this to me.) All of my equipment, with the exception of my lights, fits into it. Thus I have two units to my setup. I have seen many types of easels and some of them have splendid ideas for construction. My purpose here is not to underestimate the value of others, but rather encourage you to get yours built and soon learn that your chalk can talk.

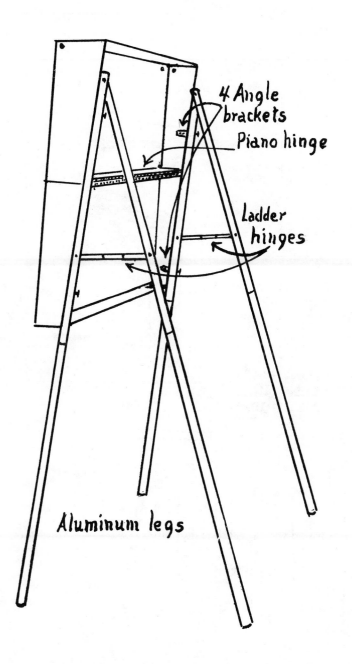

4 Angle
brackets

Piano hinge

Ladder
hinges

Aluminum legs

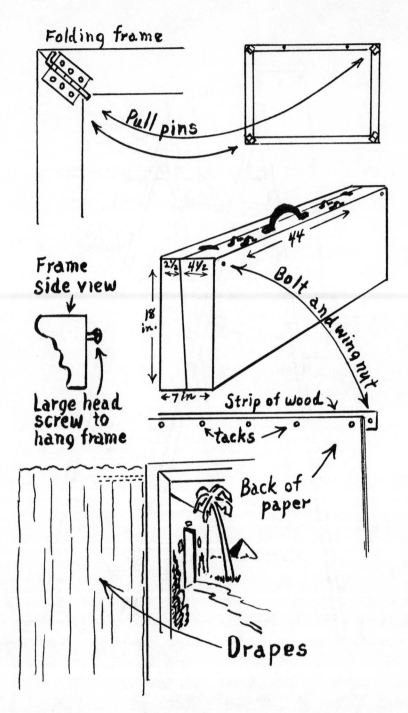

Folding frame

Pull pins

Frame
side view

Large head
screw to
hang frame

44

2½ 4½

18
in.

7in

Bolt and wing nut

Strip of wood

tacks

Back of
paper

Drapes

Chalk tray

Bolt and wing nut

Some ideas

Heavy Metal Base

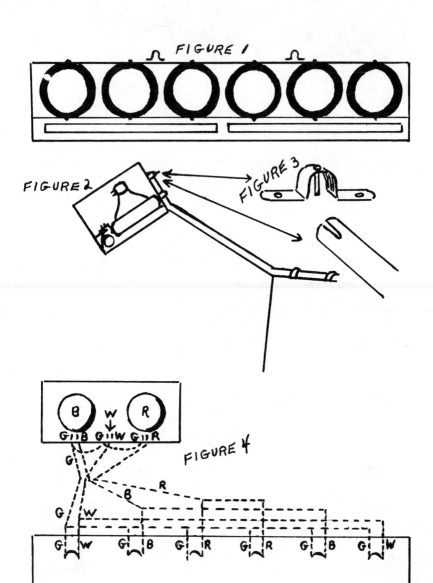

FIGURE 1

FIGURE 2

FIGURE 3

FIGURE 4

54

EASEL LIGHTING

A series of floodlights should be part of your equipment and arranged well above and out from the front of the easel. I have six (Fig. 1) 150-watt bulbs, 120 volts. About the most compact bulb of this power is the PAR 38 GE Compact Projector Flood — Code 150 Par/3 FL — 0690. Rather than a screw-in type, it has two prongs to which the wires are soldered (Fig. 2). This leaves the bulb free to swivel in the bracket that holds the bulb (Fig. 2). These brackets are colored lens holders and can be bought at an electrical store. With these holders, light can be directed to any part of the easel. Large screw-in type bulbs are bulky.

Color wheels are used successfully. One must, however, be careful to concentrate the colored light on the easel *only*.

Clear (drawing) lights should be at either end of the shield to give full benefit of light to the drawing area.

Light shields should be made carefully of aluminum by a tinsmith. The dimensions of mine are 37" x 7" x 6."

Inside the same shield I have attached my black-light fixture (Fig. 1). For various sizes and power to fit your need, consult catalog of Ultraviolet Products, Inc., 5114 Walnut Grove Avenue, San Gabriel, California 91776.

The light arrangement can be secured to the easel in various ways. Heavy brass or some other strong metal should be used (Fig. 3). Brass pipe and pipe straps are used.

In Figure 4, note the hookup from the lights to the rheostats or control board. One with a little electrical know-how can wire it.

Black-light wire is separate. Rheostats can be ordered at electrical stores.

CHALK

For colored chalk-talk pictures, lecture crayon is used. This comes in a variety of colors and can be obtained at most fully equipped art stores. One can also order from J. K. Gill Company, S.W. 5th and Stark, Portland, Oregon 97204, or Stationers Corporation, 525 South Spring Street, Los Angeles, California 90013 (order COD). The size is 1 x 1 x 3 inches. If possible buy these chalks over the counter. There are times when small hard white specks are found in the chalk; these tend to scratch the paper. Make sure your chalk is free of this and is soft.

A suede brush will take off any hard outer coating on the chalk. Sandpaper can also be used.

ULTRAVIOLET CHALK

Ultraviolet or black-light chalk comes in the same size, 1 x 1 x 3. There are two kinds of ultraviolet chalk, visible and invisible. The colors in visible ultraviolet chalk can be seen as in the plain lecture crayon. However, under the black light they become alive and vivid. One can purchase these from J. K. Gill, Stationers Corporation and any other fully equipped art stores. These are made by the American Crayon Company and are called Excello Squares.

Invisible and visible chalk can be bought at Ultraviolet Products, Inc., 5114 Walnut Grove Avenue, San Gabriel, California 91776. Hidden scenes and unusual effects can be achieved with the invisible chalks. I would advise sending to this address for their catalog on the chalk and prices. Keep in mind that ultraviolet (long wave) light is needed for this chalk.

The catalog will also suggest the ultraviolet coverage area necessary for your easel.

Avoid using Purple X bulbs because of the extreme heat they produce.

PAPER

Gray bogus paper is a good medium to use for chalk-talks. This can be purchased from Triquet Paper Company, 201 North Hosmer Street, Lansing, Michigan 48912.

This paper comes 40 x 54 inches. Order full size and cut to fit your easel. I often use leftover pieces for smaller pictures. Avoid paying postage for scraps. One hundred sheets minimum order. For economy, share your order with another chalk artist. No COD. Send for price list.

Try erasing your pictures each time. I use a small hand vacuum cleaner and a heavy blackboard eraser. As a result, the paper develops a very good tooth or blending surface. When beginning a new sheet, scuff up the surface (rough side) with a suede brush or sandpaper. Brush off excess dust.

NEWSPRINT

At your local newspaper office you should be able to acquire ends of rolls with many yards of paper. Cut this to size for cartoons, diagrams or any of the simple drawings given in this book. Tack about a dozen sheets on your easel for drawing cushion. Pads of newsprint or similar paper in various sizes can be obtained at fully equipped art stores.

One can use bright colored chalks on newsprint to a good advantage (children are attracted to colors), but blending does not work too well. Generally it is best to outline colors with black. Fold corners of newsprint for quick tear-off.

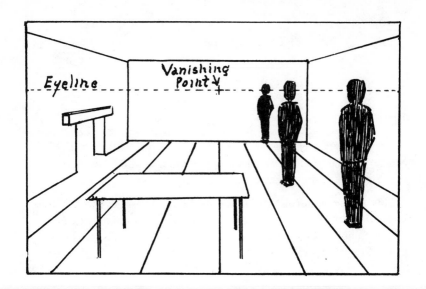

Eyeline

Vanishing Point ✗

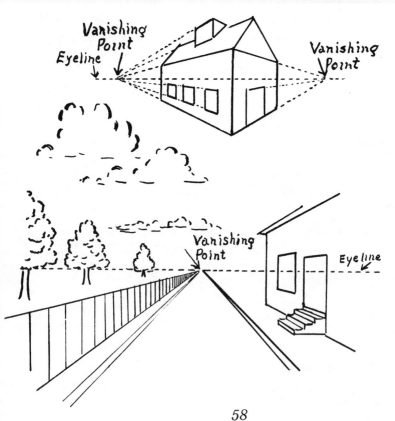

Vanishing Point
Eyeline

Vanishing Point

Vanishing Point

Eyeline

58

PERSPECTIVE

A working knowledge of this subject is a must for all chalk-talkers. The flat surface of our easel must show some objects far away and some close. How can we draw distance in our pictures?

The answer is — perspective.

We must first understand important lines such as horizontal lines, parallel lines, vertical lines, inclined lines, etc.

Study the illustrations on the opposite page. The object (clouds also) appear smaller as they recede from you. The parallel lines appear to meet at what is called the vanishing point on the eye-line or horizon line. This horizon line is always at the eye level. This is true regardless how high or low we are. Objects at a different angle will have their own vanishing point on the eyeline. This is called angular perspective.

You can develop a feeling of perspective in landscapes or sea-scapes. Delicate colors as light blue or light purple tend to suggest distance. Bold colors bring objects close.

When I was a lad, I often amused myself with a magazine and a ruler. It was fun to check up on the perspective of the illustrator. Try it sometime and find that vanishing point.

COMPOSITION AND BALANCE

The Apostle Paul in Ephesians 4:15-16 presents to us a wonderful definition of composition and balance. Christ is the main center of interest and we, members of his body "*fitly* joined together. . . ." May we "grow up" and find this to be a reality.

The word "composition" simply means the arrangement of the objects in your picture. This also involves placing one object over another. One cannot make a strict rule for composition. Through continual drawing, you will develop a sense of proper balance and composition.

I trust the few hints following will be helpful. (Notice the viewfinder on page 22.) Here is an idea for selecting a good composition:

Divide masses equally from the center of your picture. Keep the drawing from being lopsided or top-heavy. A good composition is one where everything in the drawing is subordinate to the center of interest.

Since colored chalk pictures begin with *distant* objects, keep in mind that your foreground needs to be bold enough to suggest dimension.

Generally it is better to place the horizon line above or below the center of your drawing.

Uniformity of trees, clouds, and the sawtooth type mountains will give your picture an unnatural look.

Keep your main subject large enough to be appreciated by viewers farthest from you.

Avoid objects of equal size drawn in the same area of your picture.

A picture is dull when all objects drawn are horizontal. A sweeping cloud or the tilt of the foreground will break the montony.

Guard against lines that meet and travel in the same direction.

Since chalk pictures should be done in a minimum of time, unnecessary details must be eliminated.

PROGRAM BACKGROUNDS

Music and art blend well in presenting the gospel. This gives us the advantage of reaching people through the ear-gate and the eye-gate at the same time.

Musical instruments should not be played in such a way as to detract from the drawing. The musician should prayerfully choose songs that fit the message in the picture.

I have prepared tapes having a good variety of gospel selections, including poems that fit certain chalk-talks. These tapes can be made up on various themes, such as: Calvary, the Good Shepherd, Heaven, the Resurrection, etc.

Appropriate Scriptures and poetry, read or recited, will also leave effective impressions. Keep in mind the development of each phase of the picture as you arrange your background music. Try to finish both picture and music at the same time. The last selection should have a strong suggestion of the theme.

Hanging the frame, or some other quiet signal can be given to those supplying background. If possible, they should be in a position where they can watch the drawing.

Always remember to acknowledge those assisting you.

Keep a record of your pictures in a small loose-leaf notebook. Number and name each picture. Register your drawing, when and where given.

Have several sheets of paper on your easel. This will act as a cushion for your drawing surface.

Try using rubber gloves when drawing. They should fit snugly on the hand. Put talcum powder on hands first. Your hands will be clean when handling your Bible. Washing hands or using waterless soap is messy.

Gray bogus paper is much better for drawing when first scuffed up with sandpaper or a suede brush.

A verticle picture would be a refreshing change. This could be done by fastening your paper vertically on the easel.

I have found that some purple has a tendency to fade to a light gray after a period of time.

Try ultraviolet white on white newsprint for a surprise. A black light is needed, of course.

Try brushing out pictures. Wipe off chalk with a chalkboard eraser. A hand vacuum cleaner is handy to use in brushing out pictures. Use the hand vacuum to clean eraser. Brushing out pictures will give your paper excellent tooth.

Color wheels are inexpensive and are fairly effective.

In spraying your pictures, be careful not to glob the liquid in one place. Often, spraying will deaden your brilliant colors.

A piece of felt makes a good blending tool.

Carry a light drop cloth with you. Falling chalk could harm platform rugs.

Fold ends of newsprint for quick tear-off.

Avoid using thumbtacks.

Masking tape is indispensable.

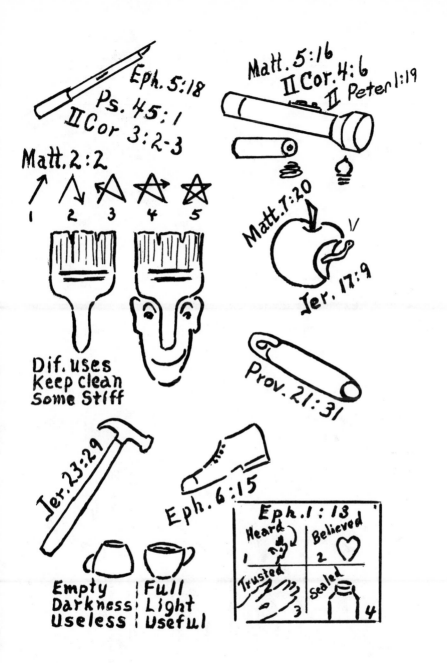

Eph. 5:18
Ps. 45:1
II Cor 3:2-3

Matt. 5:16
II Cor. 4:6
II Peter 1:19

Matt. 2:2

1   2   3   4   5

Matt. 7:20

Jer. 17:9

Dif. uses
Keep clean
Some Stiff

Prov. 21:31

Jer. 23:29

Eph. 6:15

Empty   Full
Darkness   Light
Useless   Useful

Eph. 1:13
Heard   Believed
1   2
Trusted   Sealed
      3   4

Red
Orange
Yellow
Green
Blue
Purple

Rainbow Colors

PARDON

Isa. 55:7
micah 7:18+19

SINS